T0193406

SECOND CHANCE FIRST IMPRESSION

*10 Steps to Reach Your Destiny
and Understand Your Purpose*

IRENE PEARSON

authorHOUSE®

AuthorHouse™
1663 Liberty Drive
Bloomington, IN 47403
www.authorhouse.com
Phone: 833-262-8899

Published by AuthorHouse 09/15/2023

ISBN: 979-8-8230-1468-7 (sc)
ISBN: 979-8-8230-1466-3 (hc)
ISBN: 979-8-8230-1467-0 (e)

Library of Congress Control Number: 2023917450

Print information available on the last page.

Any people depicted in stock imagery provided by Getty Images are models,
and such images are being used for illustrative purposes only.
Certain stock imagery © Getty Images.

Scripture quotations marked KJV are from the Holy Bible, King James Version
(Authorized Version). First published in 1611. Quoted from the KJV Classic
Reference Bible, Copyright © 1983 by The Zondervan Corporation.

This book is printed on acid-free paper.

Because of the dynamic nature of the Internet, any web addresses or links contained in
this book may have changed since publication and may no longer be valid. The views
expressed in this work are solely those of the author and do not necessarily reflect the
views of the publisher, and the publisher hereby disclaims any responsibility for them.

To the God of Israel, and my savior, Jesus Christ, who gives me strength.

To my parents, Mary Frances and Willie James Pearson; my aunties Carrie Massey and Joann Arant; my children Larry, Shakeba, Joshua, and Erica.

And to the only siblings I have left, Cynthia and Donald Pearson.

In honor of my late siblings: James Tillman, Gary Pearson, Willie Ann Pearson, and Lucille Pearson and grandchildren.

Also to my entire family, who love and encourage me.

I extend this book as part of our legacy for the next generation to carry on.

CONTENTS

FOREWORD

Second chances are something that we all hope for. They offer us opportunities to redeem ourselves, make up for a lost time, or start over. But all too often, we let our fear of failure stand in the way of taking advantage of second chances.

Many people go through life feeling like they missed out on something. They think that because they didn't have the perfect childhood or the perfect parents, they're doomed to lives of mediocrity. But that's not true. Everyone has the opportunity to create his or her own success story, no matter what an individual's past may be.

Irene is a living proof of this. She's been divorced twice and had to raise her children as a single parent. But she never gave up on her dreams and goals. In fact, she used her experiences to fuel her success.

If Irene can do it, anyone can.

Irene's story proves that it's never too late to start living your best life. You can always turn things around, no matter your age or circumstances.

In this book, Irene shares how you can overcome

adversity and offers inspiration and advice for anyone facing challenges in life.

Whether you're starting over after a divorce, facing unemployment, or simply feeling like you're not where you want to be, Irene's story proves that it's never too late to turn things around. This book is for anyone who feels like they've missed their chance at life. It's never too late to start fresh and make a great first impression. So let Irene show you how it's done.

So if you've been given a second chance, don't let it go to waste. Use it as an opportunity to finally achieve your dreams. And if you're unsure where to start, pick up a copy of Irene's book.

Written By: Ovie Success

ACKNOWLEDGMENT

This book wouldn't have been possible without me acknowledging the people who have poured into my life.

I first give honored to my Lord and Savior Jesus Christ, for giving me the strength, the idea, the willingness, and the desire to write and finish this book.

I also want to thank the most precious people in my life, my mom, Mary Frances Pearson, and my dad, Willie James Pearson, who took great care of me, loved, and protected me, who always had my back, and made sure that my needs were met.

I want to thank my children for sticking by me, believing in me, and continuing to give me love, support, and hope.

I am grateful for the love, care, and emotional support of my family and friends who never fail to make me laugh.

I especially want to thank my late spiritual dad and mom, Apostle Chester Nubine Jr. and Bishop Bobbie Smith, who have both passed away. You are truly missed. I appreciate them for pouring into me and speaking God's divine purpose for my life, along with teaching me spiritual things, and the ways of God. I am also thankful that God was able to use them to speak life into my future. I hope and pray that I can pour into others, the way you have poured into me. I know you are in heaven, and I believe that I will see you again one day with the Father.

I want to thank Apostle Delphene Morris, and your prayer team for your moral, spiritual support and inspiration and for allowing God to use you to ordain me as an evangelist. I thank the Lord for your powerful teachings and the wisdom that you have bestowed upon me. You are a true woman of God. May the Lord continue to bless you and your ministry.

To Bishop Peter and Pastor Sarah Morgan, whom I have sat under for years and got great teachings and spiritual instructions, I thank you for the impartation and display of wisdom.

Giving honor to Pastor Nelson, at Church of the Anointing, who is a powerful and faithful man of God. I truly thank you for spiritually watching over my children whom I have kept in church all their lives, because God said to train up a child in the way he should go, and when he is old, he won't depart. I brought them as far as I could, and I thank God for using you to take them farther. May God truly bless you and your ministry.

While there are so many more, I can't forget Pastor Rochelle Nooner, Evangelist Jacqueline Herrera, Dr. Jynona Norwood, whom the Lord has used mightily in my life. Thank you for your prayers, encouragement, wisdom, and instructions.

And to all of the spiritual leaders, and mentors such as Arthur Weiss, "A very wise man," and dear friend, who nurtured me with wisdom, and to all that have poured into my life, both directly and indirectly, you know who you are. I can't name them all but, I truly thank you.

A special thanks to all of the women that I've named.

I wish I could be half the woman that you are. You are my "sheroes."

A very special thank you to my neighbors who constantly encouraged me to finish this book.

I would like to extend a special thanks to each and every one of you.

I want you to know that I stand on your shoulders.

I stand on your shoulders for the strength that you've given me.

I stand on your shoulders for moral support.

I stand on your shoulders for your inspiration and teachings.

I stand on your shoulders for the experience, and I thank you for believing in me and seeing in me what I didn't see in myself and your love.

I hope this book will bring you joy knowing that the love, direction, experience, and teachings that you've extended in my life didn't go to waste.

And to everyone who purchases and reads this book: My sincere gratitude goes out to you for your support believing in me, and trusting me enough to speak into your life, and share my experiences with you. I hope and pray that you find what you need as you go on your journey to your destiny, purpose, and success.

And last but not least, I want to thank Author House Publishing for getting me through this process, and encouraging me to keep moving forward to completion. Much love to you all!

INTRODUCTION

The title of my book, *Second Chance First Impression*, brings to mind the question: How does one not make a good first impression?

In many cases, it's a result of being misunderstood or not prepared, even though, regardless of how smart you are, you lack the credentials to show it.

Maybe you gained a little weight, and somehow they misjudged you, couldn't see the real you. Or maybe it was just the wrong time.

You may have missed out on making a good first impression for a variety of reasons, or it might have happened more than once throughout your life.

Despite knowing that you've always been unique and special, you may not have reached your full potential. Even though you've always felt great, maybe you were afraid you wouldn't have the chance if you didn't act now. Because of this, it may cause some anxiety because you once had dreams and hopes shattered by circumstances, and so much time has passed.

It's natural for you to feel sadness and emptiness regarding greatness, but this time must be taken in order to learn your craft so that when it's born, it won't be premature. You may have felt emptiness, a sense of losing out, so why not take advantage of life to the fullest, right?

It doesn't matter that life's unpredicted circumstances have led you in a different direction, your dream is still alive, and you can reach your dreams and goals, even if you feel like your expectations have drowned.

It's not too late for you, my friend. Your mission remains to let the world see who you truly are and achieve what you've set out to accomplish.

It's my hope that this book will assist you in discovering your greatness and eliminating the fear that comes with not knowing how, when, and where to succeed as you continue on your journey.

There's an old saying: "You never get a second chance to make a first impression."

Well, it's not always the case if you don't allow it.

Because understanding your purpose is the key to reaching your destiny, understanding your true value, and your self-worth, and what you can offer the world.

Identify who you are, who God has created differently and wants to make a difference in someone's life. He has given you the gift to accomplish that mission.

Throughout this book, you'll discover that you've always had the power and the keys to unlock your destiny. It's your birthright to win with the gift that God has given you.

Remember: your destiny is waiting on you!

Chapter 1

FINDING MY PASSION

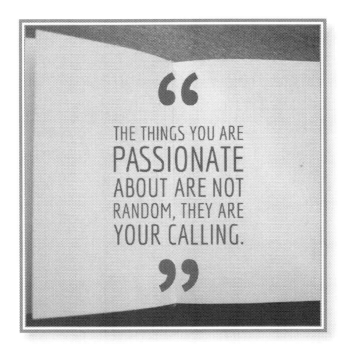

> THE THINGS YOU ARE **PASSIONATE** ABOUT ARE NOT RANDOM, THEY ARE **YOUR CALLING.**

*A*s I was writing this book, I was taken me back in my mind to my hometown in North Carolina. And I remembered my late sister Ann, who had a voice like an angel, and the amazing experience she had on my life.

She could hold notes that ran up and down a scale,

and she was sometimes called Aretha Franklin or Patti LaBelle.

She inspired me so much. And because of that, I always wanted to sing, not particularly like her, but just to sing.

So every day after school, I would practice singing. And she would come in later, always giggling when she passed the room. But I didn't let that stop me because I knew that if I just kept trying, I would sing someday.

So I kept trying, and one day, there was a talent show at our school. It was a talent show that my sister didn't enter—otherwise, I wouldn't even have tried. Oh no, not for her to blow me out of the water!

So I proceeded to enter the talent show. And guess what. I won! And she had to have been somewhere in the audience or heard about it. Because when she came home, she said to me, "Um, you finally learned how to sing."

She was like my mentor, and I really looked up to her.

And we should always have a mentor, someone we can look up to, someone who has our back, and someone who believes in us. Because as the years passed, my voice developed. And whenever I had any difficulty with a song, I would call her. She would give me advice, and I would always be able to get through it.

Then one day, I asked her who her favorite singer

was. And she said it was me! That really surprised me. It made me so proud to hear my sister say that, because she was such a great singer. And it inspired me to realize that I could do and be whatever I wanted and set my mind to.

You should also identify what is inside of you and ignites your passion, the thing that drives you. You won't have to look far because it screams inside of you every day.

But it's also important to have a support system. Many of my friends from my hometown always expected me to succeed in California. And they didn't hear from me about my singing career for years. But occasionally, someone would ask me about it, and that kept me inspired. But my life took another turn.

Before I went to California, I had my first son, Larry, at an early age. So I didn't finish high school, but I still had the desire to go to California and become a singer.

But there were so many things happening in California, and I didn't really take singing seriously when I moved there. In the years that followed, I missed many opportunities that came my way. And nine years later, I had my second child, Shakeba. Then I got married and had Joshua and Erica.

As time passed, I divorced my husband, became a single mom with four children, and was homeless. Now what could I do to take care of them?

During that period, it was quite challenging, as you can imagine. There were many nights when I had to sleep in my car. Thankfully, the shelter provided me with excellent resources, including a well-planned entrance and exit strategy. Through the shelter, I had access to job placement services, computer training, and so much more! This experience gave me a deeper understanding and empathy for what homeless individuals go through and how I can better assist them in the future.

That's where I was able to acquire my insurance licensed. I came to the realization that I could fulfill my life's purpose. To achieve my goals, I made the most of every opportunity that came my way. I also had the ability to braid and weave hair, so I started braiding hair. And as soon as I was able to, I put my family in an apartment. Then, after taking stockbroker classes and obtaining my insurance license, I still didn't really know what I wanted to do. As a result, I was inspired to pursue another journey that I was very passionate about, namely, my interest in promotion and marketing.

I had never looked at billboards or ads on TV the same way that most people do. I always wanted to know how the advertising was designed and why they promoted the products the ways that they did. And the type of music they used in commercials it always intrigued and fascinated me. So watch out for these signs because that might be a key to revealing your destiny and purpose.

In my hometown, I used to organize talent shows. It wasn't until I hosted an event at the Los Angeles Convention Center that I discovered my passion for advertising, promotions, and marketing. This led me to become an independent agent, where I worked on promoting and marketing various products. Eventually, I started my own business and built a street team to help me promote products and services for different companies. We also engage in community outreach work within our local area.

At that point, I felt that I really could make it on my own. But despite my dream of doing big things in advertising, promotions, and marketing, I could only see the big picture. I didn't realize that I had to start small and work my way up.

And because I was eager to reach what I was seeing, I didn't realize how to get there.

And we may often think that we're going in the wrong direction, or it's taking longer than we expect. But like the GPS on a freeway, God knows how to keep us on track, even when we make mistakes.

The only way to get to what you truly see in this life is to take baby steps. Then you won't get frustrated trying to get there.

Because I wanted it now, it was difficult to do anything to raise the money I needed. Even if I had to work at a fast-food restaurant or babysit, it always seemed long-term.

It would have been nice if I had known then what I know now. How many of us have said that?

But I still had bills to pay.

I then realized that I finally had to get in gear and do what I needed to do, which can be frustrating if you're not prepared to wait and be diligent.

We must be patient with our visions, dreams, and destinies. And always remember: your destiny is waiting on you.

The road to success may be paved with ups and downs and lots of pitfalls. But just be patient—success will happen eventually!

Having made bad choices in the past, I no longer blame myself for not moving forward or being more successful sooner.

Remember that no matter what we have to endure in life, if we trust in God, we will be able to continue the plan. However, we must rely completely on him.

In this book, I'm going to give you ten steps to reaching your destiny and understanding your purpose.

In the chapters moving forward, you'll learn how to break the myth that you can never get a second chance to make a first impression, how to realize that you are good enough, and how to never give up.

Always remember: destiny is waiting for you!

Quiz

- Why is it a good idea to have a mentor?
- What is the importance of having a support system?
- What are the reasons you should pay attention to signs and signals around you in your daily life?

Chapter 2

PREPARATION

$\mathcal{W}$HAT IS PREPARATION, SOME MAY ask.

Preparation is the action or process of making ready or being made ready for use or consideration.

The thing you want is waiting for you in the right place. You just have to find it and connect with it. And as I said earlier, it's all about that burning desire.

I'll continue to ask you this question because I want it to get into your spirit. There may be something inside of you that keeps eating at you, a burning desire that won't let go, or a knowing that's deep inside.

This is the first thing that you'll notice about your destiny.

You may not understand why you have this feeling, but pay attention. That burning desire will lead you to your purpose.

The destiny that God has given you is what I believe your purpose in life is.

Everyone has a gift. And according to Proverbs 18:16,

A man's gift maketh room for him, and bringeth him before great men.

When you discover what your gift is, you'll find your destiny and purpose.

> At that point, you will need to write the vision and make it plain upon tables, that he may run that readeth it. (Habakkuk 2:2)

Everything you see on this earth was first a thought, and a vision, before it became a reality. Someone saw it, spoke it, and then it became a reality.

> And Jesus answering saith unto them, "Have faith in God. For verily I say unto you, That whosoever shall say unto this mountain, 'Be thou removed, and be thou

cast into the sea'; and shall not doubt in his heart, but shall believe that those things which he saith shall come to pass; he shall have whatsoever he saith. Therefore I say unto you, What things soever ye desire, when ye pray, believe that ye receive them, and ye shall have them." (Mark 11:22–24)

And a dream may seem impossible, bigger than you, or out of reach. But it's a daily confession that you have to make to yourself to guide you toward achieving it.

It may seem impossible at first, and you may even find it intimidating. But the vision you have is exactly what you were built for. You need to see it through God's lens as he shows it to you.

And you have to speak it in the universe. God first spoke it, and it became what he said. He has given you the same ability to see and believe it, but we have to see it first to achieve it.

After you know what it is—what it can do for you— it's time to act and be prepared. Most people's biggest challenge is starting, once they know what it can do.

How Do I Prepare?

Be sure to first do your research and find out who your market is and who your competitors are. Don't be concerned about others doing the same thing.

Their visions are different from yours, so yours will be unique.

It's important to set goals about what you need to do first, next, and last in order to prepare.

In the next few pages of this chapter, I'm going to show you practical ways to prepare.

First, we want to make sure that our minds are fed with as much information as possible so that we can boost our progress and make the best decisions in the pursuit of our goals. This will be accomplished in your research.

It's important to always know that we should lead by example and make the best of any situation, especially when it comes to helping others or achieving our goals by staying ahead of the game.

By using the principle of preparation, you should always be ready and efficient for anything that comes your way, prepare ahead of time, and leave the least complex tasks to do last.

Always prioritize what's most important because everything needs to be well prepared and then on what kind of planning works best for you, because it keeps you in control of what you want and need to do every day.

It should be well thought out and prepared because if you want to succeed in anything, preparation is your most important asset, so it needs to be done over and over, step by step, if you want to be successful.

In order to stay ahead of the game, we must always plan ahead and prepare for the future.

It's imperative that we stay focused and visualize our progress towards our goals; otherwise, we won't succeed in achieving them.

Keep the picture before you to help you stay focused on your goals and visualize that you are actually doing it successfully.

We must be prepared as Paul writes in 2 Timothy 4:2, "Preach the word. Be ready to do it whether it is convenient or inconvenient, correct, confront, and encourage with patience and instruction."

So sometimes it's not going to feel good. You may not feel like you have no energy to move another step. But keep moving because it's a small price to pay to reach your goal, so be consistent.

In addition, remember that we must practice constantly.

My mother used to say, practice makes perfect, and I have found that to be true in my life as well.

There's a difference between preparing for something and planning for it. Planning is something different from preparing for something.

Here are the definitions:

- Preparation finds the most efficient way to do things.
- Planning is the process of making plans for something.

We strive to keep the two distinct. Stay focused on your plan and goals, prepare every day, and always keep an understanding of what your goals are. Research and read everything that has to do with your goals, and always know what the purpose of your plan is.

The best way to succeed in any project or plan is to become a master strategist, constantly strategizing how to get through each phase.

In addition to avoiding pitfalls and avoiding losing out, preparing beforehand could benefit you in a variety of other ways as well.

Listed below are some examples of what we do every day to prepare.

- prayer
- cleaning
- staying fit by exercising
- getting up early to be on time for school or work
- meal planning
- preparation for a meeting
- studying for an examination

In addition to all of these, there are so many others.

Now, let's talk about planning for our futures. Here in this chapter, I've given you several examples that you can apply to any type of planning. However, we often don't take this part of our plans seriously enough, that we may not be able to support the next generation adequately.

What Are Your Plans for the Future?

In every case, the steps may differ depending on what you're doing, whether you're preparing for retirement or child care, personal, business, or estate planning.

In order to achieve the goal of that plan, we need to find ways and solutions to achieve it, and in this example, it's important to save for your future by coming up with a plan, and then working that plan.

So in this case you may want to consider getting a

financial planner. Financial planners can be very useful and beneficial.

Duties of a Financial Planner

The role of a financial planner is to help clients create long-term financial plans by offering broad financial advice, or by specializing in one area, such as investments, taxes, retirement, or estate planning.

Keeping this in mind when making our plans towards our destiny is something we should not overlook.

In the next chapter, I will guide you through achieving this.

Quiz

- What does preparation mean to you?
- What is the first thing you would notice about your destiny?
- What will be your steps to staying detailed oriented?
- Why is it important to prepare?
- What is that burning desire inside of you that won't let you quit?

Chapter 3

SETTING SMALL GOALS

Goals

$\mathcal{D}$REAMS AND GOALS MAY SEEM the same, but you need to be more specific about what you want to accomplish and when you want the task completed. Your goal should be broken down into three parts to stay on course.

When setting goals, it's important to make them measurable, achievable, and written. It's also recommended to set both short-term, medium-term, and long-term goals. This is because setting goals requires precision and prioritization. To start, write down a small goal, a medium goal, and an overall goal. Once you've determined your goals, begin by focusing on the small ones. As a simple example of losing weight, let's say you want to lose fifty pounds. Your small goal would be to lose around two to three pounds a week or a month.

To accomplish that, you'll need to monitor your diet and develop a meal plan.

No matter what your goals are, don't beat yourself up if you aren't able to accomplish it at that point. You did well if you accomplished most of it, and you should be able to achieve your ultimate goal soon, because this is a process that will lead to your success.

While we're discussing dieting in this example, you can use it for anything, whether it's business or personal.

I learned that working hard and staying determined will eventually get me to where I want to be by staying focused. Working hard every day on my goal motivated me, and I have lost more than fifty pounds in 6 months by designing a meal plan and changing my old eating habits.

Keep at it, and you'll get there. If I couldn't do just one thing a day toward my goals, I would feel terrible, but if I could do just one thing a day, I'd already be closer to achieving them.

A Dream

Dreams, however, I believe, are what I believe God places in our hearts, those things we crave that nudge us and make us want to reach our goals. It's the desire that tugs at our spirit to succeed. The dream may be to become a great basketball player, a great singer, a nurse, or perhaps to open a daycare center.

So, whatever that dream is, I believe that's your purpose and destiny. No dream is too small or less important, someone always need what you have to offer, and remember: he said in Habakkuk 2:3,

> For the vision is yet for an appointed time, but at the end it shall speak, and not lie: though it tarry, wait for it; because it will surely come, it will not tarry.

Always seek him for clarity and directions. Just understand that you need to see the end result every day in your mind and spirit. By doing these things and practicing these behaviors, you'll feel more motivated to continue moving forward. For example, you might hang pictures on your walls, look in a book for notes, or look back at what you have accomplished.

Once you realize you've accomplished so much, you'll be inspired to go even further.

At the time, it may not seem like you're doing

anything, but know that every day you do something, you're getting closer, and one day you'll look back and realize it was all worth it.

You'll accomplish it one day at a time if you don't give up, and don't feel overwhelmed or intimidated with the task. You can look at other resources and people who have achieved similar success in your field to encourage you.

Don't be afraid to ask questions. Keep a daily journal and a thing-to-do notepad. Mark off daily what has been done. This will also keep you motivated and remind you to do something daily.

Stay positive because preparation and opportunity is a winning combination. You must be prepared to succeed from the beginning to the end.

As our friend Zig Ziglar said best, Success occurs when opportunity meets preparation. Source: By: Good Reads.

Regardless of our situation, we should strive to enhance and excel in our pursuits. It's possible that some of us may be uncertain about our genuine passions, strengths, or objectives. Therefore, it's essential to allocate time for self-reflection to determine what we aspire to accomplish.

When you discover that, try to accomplish the skills to achieve it. There are many ways to find out how to accomplish a skill or gain knowledge in today's world on the superhighway of the internet.

There's so much information. We are flooded with it every day. So it's not as hard as it used to be for our grandparents. It's very easy to find what we need and want to do.

Watching and learning from others can spark creativity and inspire fresh ideas that are unique to your own interests. If you have a vision that resonates with you, pursue it with determination and gather as much information as you can to reach your goal. Remember that we all learn from each other every day. It helps us to become responsible people when we set goals and act on them. It gives us something we want to wake up for and live for.

It gives us a sense of belonging and self-worth, and we won't feel bad when we see others accomplishing what they have, with you thinking that you've been left behind.

In this way, we gain a sense of responsibility and stop blaming others for our failures because we see that the power is also within us, where we no longer have to feel inferior with others.

We learn from experience, whether it's good or bad, so we'll know what to do, what not to do, when and where to do it, and how, and we can also learn from others.

And it's not just about learning from other people's mistakes, but also about learning from other people's good decisions. If we see family and friends make good decisions and they work out, we'll be inspired to make good decisions ourselves.

To reach your destination, you must stay focused and never stop learning, be a great listener, and let go of the negative things that have happened in your life. Let go of the past and start fresh by being creative and keeping positive energy in the atmosphere around yourself.

It might seem that setting goals is just getting an idea in one's head and writing it down step by step, but I think that it encompasses much more.

I also believe that how we treat or respond to others plays a crucial role in achieving our goals.

We can get irritated just by small things that people say, and then we won't be able to reach our goals because we're now angry or depressed, making it impossible for us to think clearly. So we must surround ourselves with positive people who have positive energy and keep that energy around us all the time.

This will keep you on track so your thoughts and your creativity can flourish. Never take anything or anyone for granted, always remember: To take what is granted to you for granted, it will be taken from you (Actress Sonia Uchie)

Getting started can be challenging, especially if you're setting small goals. In order to get into the right frame of mind, we must make sure that we have everything in order around us. It takes time and effort to get our minds in the right place. Getting in gear for our plan requires ensuring all the things in our lives that need to be corrected are done.

Note: Clean the house first. Then you can put in the new furniture.

And last but not least, we want to build a legacy for our children's children.

The Bible tells us in Proverbs 13:22 (KJV), "A good man leaveth an inheritance to his children's children: and the wealth of the sinner is laid up for the just."

So if you set yourself up now you can secure the future for many generations to come. If some of our ancestors would have had this opportunity maybe a lot of us wouldn't have gone through what we have experienced.

> Train up a child in the way he should go:
> and when he is old, he will not depart from
> it.(Proverbs 22:6 KJV)

As a result, all the knowledge, skills, and experiences that we acquire, both spiritually and naturally, we should pass the plan on to our children so they can carry them on throughout their generations. Not for money only, but also for knowledge.

> A scorner seeketh wisdom, and findeth
> it not: but knowledge is easy unto him that
> understandeth. (Proverbs 14:6)

Quiz

- How can you be precise with your goals?
- What is the difference between dreams and goals?
- What are two winning combinations?
- What happens to us when we become responsible people?
- What is the best thing about our past experiences?

Chapter 4

DON'T MISS YOUR MOMENT

*T*IME IS VITALLY IMPORTANT.

Don't Miss Your Moment

We need to take advantage of every opportunity and never stop learning. Don't get comfortable with what we're doing; we never know when an opportunity will arise.

The key is to be open and prepared for it when it comes, because you never know when you'll need it or who you'll meet who can make a difference in your life.

We all like to spend time with our friends and do things together, but sometimes they might not have our best interests in mind.

That's not to say that they're bad, but you can't bring everyone with you. You have your path, and they have theirs, and they might not have the same interests, which could slow you down.

The best time to act is now, and there may never be a better moment. You don't want to waste any more time and have any regrets, meaning don't put it off for a later date.

There have been many times in my life that I have missed opportunities because of my own creative circumstances and doubt that I could have avoided.

But don't become stuck in stagnation or worry about missed opportunities if you've missed them; instead, learn from them and move forward.

Many times, we miss opportunities because we have tried so many things that have failed and we want to be careful this time, but we all take risks in everything we do every day.

Funny thing is, maybe this is the time or chance you should take because it could be a wonderful opportunity that you would not have had otherwise.

In order to identify opportunities when they present themselves, we must always put God first, pray for discernment, and if we have time, we can always research the product, service, or company just to make sure they're legit.

When you say, no, I'm not interested, and walk away without doing any research, always consider what you're saying no to, because you might be saying no to the right thing after all.

I remember when I was working for a telemarketing company and my friend and I were two of the top salespeople on the floor. Sometimes when we were tired of calling the leads on our lead sheets, we'd take our leads and trade them off with each other. But this particular day I was tired of calling on that lead sheet, and I was about to give it to my friend next to me, as we always did.

But as I decided to take a break, I thought, *Let me just try just one more contact, and then I'll take my break.*

As soon as I told the lead I called what I was calling for, he started asking me questions like whether he could get the cell phones at his multiple locations? how many could he get? and could he get the cell phones in multiple colors.

I was impressed by this guy's ability to understand my needs without me having to say much after calling multiple businesses. When I called his company, I

27

barely had to pitch my request to him because he was such a great candidate. I was surprised to learn that he managed over four hundred stores, which was crucial for my large order.

What if I had given that sheet to my friend next to me? I would have lost that sale. That's why we have to be careful about everything regarding our business and goals.

I'm glad I didn't take that chance, and my friend and I both marveled that day. I learned something I will use for the rest of my life.

The most important thing is to always pay attention and try again.

As long as it isn't a risk that will hurt you, life is all about risk, and no matter what, we should learn how to rebound when we miss a great opportunity.

But as I've learned in life over the years, even if I miss one opportunity, there are always other opportunities, sometimes even better, so all we have to do is be ready when the opportunity comes.

That's why this book is so important, as it will prepare us to not miss any more opportunities so that we'll achieve our goals.

It's important to realize that the strength we have to bounce back is a result of our experience and confidence that we'll succeed and get back on track.

There may have been situations where we thought

we missed out on a great opportunity but in reality, we weren't prepared mentally, spiritually, financially or with the skills to take advantage of it.

As I said, opportunities do come back, sometimes the same opportunity. Just be ready to take advantage of it.

It's possible that things that we see as failures or losses could actually be blessings in disguise.

I remember when there was a beautiful area where I wanted to move. It was really nice. I didn't have the finances at the time, but later, as the years passed, there was a bad fire in that area where everything burned down and people were burned in their cars and it was difficult to get out of that area.

While I feel bad for them and their families, I'm happy that I didn't move to that area because I was spared that tragedy.

It's also common to see people doing things in life that we believe we ought to have done, but for whatever reason, we weren't able to do it. It's very difficult to fulfill a dream now when we find out that someone else has already done it, as though, *Oh man, I can't do that now because someone else has already done it, and I can't fulfill my dream.*

But please remember this: even though you miss that opportunity to do it at that time and someone else did it later doesn't mean that you can't still do it! There are many different brands, names, and styles of cars that we see, while there are many different designs of buildings we see, as well as many different clothes designers that we wear every day, and a variety of songs we listen to.

If someone else is doing something you've always wanted to do, that doesn't mean you're excluded. You still have a chance to do that same thing since you're unique. They see it one way, you see it another way, and you can express that version in the way that you see it, or the way you want it done.

That's where you'll find your creativity, so don't let that stop you from doing whatever you want to do.

Wanting to Do Something at the Wrong Time

I believe that there is a road that will lead us to the path of success, regardless of whether we want something or to do something at the wrong time, or if it's not meant for us to have or do.

We have to learn to trust God and follow our instincts. He will guide you. If you find at any time you lack the skill to finish any part of your project or your plan, then you don't want to miss the next chapters which will guide you to your next step.

Remember: your destiny is waiting for you.

Quiz

- Do you think friends always have the same interests? If not, why?
- What do we do if we miss an opportunity?
- What do we do if we see someone do the same thing we always want to do?
- Do we quit? If not why?
- What was one of the key factors to learn about timing?
- What opportunities do you think you've missed?

Chapter 5

EMBRACE YOUR GIFTS
AND PERFECT THEM

We have to learn to embrace our gifts and cease every moment of opportunity.

How do we recognize an opportunity when it comes?

Here are a few things to consider:

- Is it worth considering?
- Is it a feasible idea?
- Is it going to make someone's life better?
- Are there any ambiguities? (Clarity)
- Does it have newsworthiness and viability?
- Is it achievable and affordable?
- Is it current?
- Would it be appropriate?
- Does it reflect the current state of affairs?
- How well will it solve problems?

By conducting research, visiting your neighborhood, or networking with other business people, you can find answers. The good news is, if you don't have the time, energy, or skills, you can always hire an expert.

It's not uncommon for business owners to hire experts in their fields because they may not have a clue about their full operations; however, since they have done their own research about their business, they're likely to know what needs to be done and how to do it, but they don't do it themselves.

In addition, you can always take classes to help you better understand your business and how it functions before you start.

Embracing and Perfecting Your Gift

Remember: God uses everything you go through in life to move you into your destiny. Nothing and no part of your mistake or success is wasted. It all works together for your good.

> And we know that all things work together for good to them that love God, to them who are the called according to his purpose. (Romans 8:28)

Stay consistent on your path. Don't get sidetracked. It's so easy to get off course. Always keep your character intact and have good integrity …

My pastor, Sarah Morgan, used to say, don't let your gift take you where your character can't keep you. Your gift may take you there, but your character will determine if you stay there.

It's important to maintain good character and act on good habits before they turn into bad ones. Don't wait for the perfect timing to make decisions - take action now and don't let procrastination become a bad habit. Time can pass by quickly, so it's important to make the most of it. Be unique.The world is tired of seeing and hearing the same thing, being different is the key.

Procrastination

Don't try to be like anyone else. You're special, and you're unique. You can't be a people pleaser and please everybody, because someone will always find a way to criticize or discredit you with an aim to stunt your growth, crush your spirit, and hope you quit.

Though we may not know our gifts and haven't discovered them yet, some of us know what our gifts are and are afraid to use them.

Get out from behind those walls and show the world your gifts, because the world needs them.

Embrace the power within, that God has placed there, it's just lying dormant until you grasp and ignite it, or it will die with you.

To procrastinate is to postpone an action or put off doing something.

Time doesn't stand still for anyone, and we are getting older every day, so don't let time pass you by causing you to live in regrets.

You can start now by taking baby steps, inch by inch, until you reach your goals. If your only obstacle is money, you can start saving even if it means taking a job you wouldn't normally do.

This should be done after you've determined how much you'll need to complete your project, buy a computer, buy a car, or whatever it is that you need to accomplish your goals.

It's advisable to have a daily action plan; this will keep you on track. Review your list weekly, check off your accomplishments, and keep track of your savings.

Always try to pay your bills on time, as you don't need to add any additional stress to your life. You must become disciplined in your spending and daily habits in order to avoid being in debt.

If there are other obstacles in your path, identify what those obstacles are and seek out a solution. The idea is to never give up.

Some Things People Do to Procrastinate and Why

People often get overly excited about their projects and waste time thinking that they have enough time, before they realize, one day, they don't.

In addition, they start telling the wrong people about their plans to the point where they feel they have to be perfect, and they're afraid of embarrassment and failure.

As a result, they have to juggle it in between their jobs, parenting, and careers since they lack the financial resources or time that can sometimes slow them down.

This is why time management is so important.

How to Persevere

To eliminate procrastination, fill your schedule with very little things to do each day. You'll need to schedule the time needed for each assignment on your schedule.

To keep the cost down, maybe you can hire a nanny family member or friend. Occasionally, you may have also put things on your to-do list until you can accomplish them or get to them later.

However, don't let it overwhelm you, you should follow up on your phone calls and emails, especially those who are waiting for your response; don't keep them waiting, be responsible.

Some Procrastination Things Are Out of Our Control

These are things such as trauma, death, mental illness, or sickness that we simply can't do anything about but to seek professional help.

What Happens to Our Brain if We Procrastinate Too Long?

Research has found that chronic procrastination is linked to low self-esteem low energy and depression.

So to avoid these events in our lives we should always stay focused and on point towards our goals.

In the next chapter you'll learn about how to do strategic planning the right way to reach your goals.

Remember: you're on a mission, and your destiny is waiting for you!

Quiz

- How do we recognize an opportunity when it comes?
- And, what are one of the key points?
- What does it mean to procrastinate?
- What are two things to do in our daily plan of action?
- What are the reasons people procrastinate?
- Give two key points on how you'll overcome procrastination.

Chapter 6

STRATEGIC PLANNING

What Does Strategic Planning Mean?

STRATEGIC PLANNING INVOLVES ESTABLISHING YOUR vision for the future as well as identifying your goals and objectives.

This process determines the order in which the goal should be achieved so that you're able to achieve your mission, once you identify what the vision of your plan is.

But please understand that planning is one thing and strategy is another. Once you get a clear understanding of what your plan is and you have written it down now it's time to get to work, this is where the big job comes in because planning is easier than strategizing.

Planning

You may not have everything in order at the beginning, but don't get discouraged. Just keep working on it, and you'll see how it grows.

> Do not despise these small beginnings, for the Lord rejoices to see the work begin, to see the plumb line in Zerubbabel's hand. (Zechariah 4:10 NLT)

Be not weary in well doing.

> And let us not be weary in well doing: for in due season we shall reap, if we faint not. (Galatians 6:9)

Stay focused on each step of your plan and don't be hard on yourself if you don't have everything in place right away.

Take a break and relax during your research to come up with fresh ideas.

Prepare beforehand for interviews or presentations. Learn about the business or subject matter in advance. Practice your scripts or presentations in front of a mirror. This will help you gain confidence.

Strategic Planning

In this procedure, the leaders of a corporation can recognize the intentions for the future of that company.

It's necessary to begin the succession process in order to achieve the corporation's intentions precisely.

The following are a few steps to strategic planning, with instructions on how to execute them, as well as how to select the steps that will be most beneficial to you.

Well, when we have plans to do something, then we should strategize how those plans are going to come out. In doing so, we need to focus our resources on things that are going to have the most impact, and make sure we have a clear direction and stay focused on our plans.

Here's how it should be done: To make it successful, you first need to review it, identify the agenda, and get the people you need to work with you. You should establish a timeline from the beginning to the end and analyze each step along the way. That is being strategic with the plan because you have to determine how it will work.

How Can It Add Value?

Choose a market that can afford what you have to offer and make sure that market is the one you are trying to reach for what they are seeking.

What about the Cost?

Regardless of your business, whether you're running a restaurant, a child care center, or simply becoming a singer, your organization needs leaders to succeed. It's essential that you have a PR team around you to help you with your career. It's also important to have good leadership around you, a marketing team and a publicist to assist you in processing your outcome.

Make sure you get people with the skills that are required to accomplish your goals to steer you in the right direction to make the right decisions. You should also analyze any objectives that may arise as you come together and sit down and plan your strategy. Your leadership team should be able to assist you as you do so.

In reality, all strategic plans may not be suitable for every situation, and it depends on what you're doing, whether it's nonprofit or for profit, or if you're doing it on your own. Each one requires a unique approach.

You should always schedule meetings for the team to come together, leadership meetings or team meetings, depending on what you're doing. Stay ahead of the competition or on par with the competition. Don't fall behind. And stay up with whatever's trending. Keep up with any new technologies. You need to stay in a mindset of strategy in every situation.

Every leader within your organization, whether it's your employer, your managers, or your sales staff, needs to be aware of where you're going and how you're going to get there, so everyone has to be on the same page.

As you come together as a leadership team, your meetings will assist you in deciding the next steps in every aspect of your plans.

As you oversee everything, you must have foresight on any risk or anything you may be going to encounter and also to prepare for improving the organization at all times. Leave the floor open for suggestions, since you aren't the only one who has a good idea.

It's amazing how many people on your team or at your company might come up with one great idea that would complete the plan.

Don't look down on anyone, because that person might be the one who gets you to the next level.

I remember there was this one young lady on my sales team, and she kept coming back asking for more order forms and supplies.

And I kept saying to myself, *Why does this girl keep coming back when she knows she's doing nothing?* Because it seemed odd how many times she kept coming back, and I misjudged her because she turned out to be the best sales rep on the team.

As a result, I learned that old saying to not judge a book by its cover, and that is very true because the way she did it, which was her style.

I thought it wasn't good enough to meet the standard of what I expected, so always make sure that you keep an eye on everyone so that they give feedback on what needs to be done because you'll be surprised to find out that they know a lot more than you thought.

It's not just a matter of throwing something together as a plan; it's a matter of strategy. It seems like they're the same but they're really not. A strategy must be well thought out to be successful, and it's, in fact, a strategy that helps you completely develop your plan.

What Is the Strategy?

Strategy is an integrative set of choices that positions you on a playing field of your choice in a way that you could win.

Why and how are you going to do it?

You must determine your why and how you'll provide your clients with a high-quality service and beat the competition.

Put yourself in the shoes of the client, the listener,

the buyer, or whatever you're accomplishing. If it's possible, how will you achieve it?

Having a clear understanding of your plan. You now need to decide how you're going to execute it every step of the way from the beginning to the end to make it successful. And in order to be successful, you need to be strategic. But read on my friend.

Please note: When planning, you control the calls. You are not the customer. You decide what happens in the organization, how many people to hire, or how you're going to do this, or that.

Now, strategy specifies the competitive outcome that involves customers. Now the work truly begins. Will your products and services be good enough for them to buy from you and to make it profitable for you?

Remember: you don't control them. At this point, they have your full attention! (The customer)

But if you have a great strategic plan, you can do it. You don't control them. You don't control the revenues. They decide if they want your product or services. So now you have to come up with the strategic plan that will entice them to want your product or service. It's all about how many bees you can attract to your honey.

I found myself doing all these plans. I thought, if I got this done and got that done and I put the whole package together, that it was a strategic plan!

But, oh, no. Little did I know, but I was only halfway,

because now I had to convince the client that I was good enough for them to want my product or service or to be my customer. How can I add value?

Through all of that, you're going to run into so much competition that's doing the same thing, so this is where being a master strategist becomes necessary because now you have to strategically find out, discover, or invent how you're going to use strategy to cause your part of service to be inviting.

Last but not least:

If you want to achieve a complete outcome, what do you want it to look like, or how do you want it to look? You may have to start at the back and bring it all the way forward to get that answer.

In my opinion, that's the way it works for me—how I want it to look.

How many people do you hope to reach, and how will you accomplish that?

And what are your strategies for getting them to do this?

There is so much more to say about this, and in your research, you can find a lot of information to get many more answers. However, I'm giving you a basic understanding of what a master strategist should be or the direction in which you should be heading.

It's really in knowing how the game is played that you can come up with your own flavor of how to do it, and as you sit down and think about your plan, you'll come up with your own way of how you can do it, to become a master strategist.

Even though it seems like the top people have thought of everything to do, believe me: you can come up with a strategy that can win and be different, and it will come from you.

It's possible that something you haven't thought of is locked inside of you. That is the master plan that you want to strategically unveil.

If you want to know if it will work, you need to put it out there. Many people have discovered a simple strategy they would never have thought would work if they hadn't just put it out there.

Sometimes it can be so simple. It doesn't even need to be great for it to work. It may just be a simple plan, and the best way to find out is to put that plan into action by taking strategic measures to make it work.

If you can't see it clearly, then I will say go back to the drawing board and redesign it for that strategy to work.

Ensure that your team is reviewing the plan to see if it's working out in the way you envisioned it. Each team member should be held accountable; you want to accomplish your goal as quickly as possible.

It will help you to get there if you are strategic in your approach.

And as I stated earlier you can always outsource your work to the professionals to help you. In the close of this, I want to give you some steps of strategic planning and recap.

Why Do You Need A Strategic Plan?

The purpose of a strategic plan is to enable you to monitor your progress to help you get to your goal. A great team that can identify with your plan of action can be a great asset to your business.

Always Set Goals

Setting goals is the process of guiding a person or group toward an effort that is intended.

Define Your Goal

Get a clear picture as to what you want to achieve. Have a daily plan of action.

The first step in your daily action plan is to always be aware and alert and focus on the plan for today, even if it takes weeks to complete it. Work on what is most important for that plan today, what is the first step and so on, until it's complete.

Develop a Support Group and Team to Help You

By working together, people are motivated to rely on one another to achieve their goals.

It would not be easy to overcome obstacles that would have gone unnoticed without a team working together.

It allows you to discuss your challenges with one another.

Implement Your Strategic Plan

Make sure you have researched before developing a successful plan.

Resources

You'll have access to all the information you need whenever you need it by creating a highly resourceful team.

Project Management

You can assign each member of your team to do a specific part of the project, such as filling in each slice of the pie until the whole pie is filled, which is an example of your company running as a whole.

Create a Timeline

What is the start and end date of your project?

When you're ready, find a PR team to help market your business. Some goals and plans don't require this, but find what you need to get started and succeed.

Now it's time to act.

Quiz

- What does strategic planning mean?
- What should you do if you're not accomplishing much in the beginning?
- What is the process of establishing a strategic plan?
- Why do you need a strategic plan?
- Why is a support group or team helpful?

Chapter 7

SETBACKS

> The COMEBACK
> is always STRONGER
> than the SETBACK

*T*HIS CHAPTER IS PROBABLY ONE of the key factors in this whole book.

Our lives are often ruined by setbacks because they prevent us from taking advantage of great opportunities. Setbacks have been proven to be one of the most important reasons why we miss out on great opportunities.

What Is a Setback?

A setback is a reversal or a check in progress.

In other words, it's a limiting event that prevents you from making progress or gaining new ground.

That can sometimes lead to procrastination or prevent the process from moving forward.

These events in your life could cause you to feel defeated, which could cause you more difficulties in your life.

The obstacles will overwhelm you, and you won't be able to overcome them or reverse the current situation.

It can become a stumbling block and cause you to be delayed.

So How Do We Prevent Setbacks from Happening?

As you continue to read this chapter, you'll see what causes setbacks and how to prevent them, and the most common ones are the following:

Toxic People and Dream Stealers

It's possible for toxic people to play a significant role in the advancement of your destiny, whether intentionally or unintentionally.

How to Identify a Toxic Person in Your Life?

We can easily identify them by realizing our energy levels are depleted and exhausted after spending time with them, and their presence vexes our spirits, causing us to become angry, sad, or depressed around them. Because they love to gossip, you should always avoid falling into that trap.

If you dread seeing them, you may want to hide and escape. It's possible for them to start trouble, and in an attempt to protect them, we end up covering for them, because they dramatize everything, and we believe them. Stop trying to impress this person because they don't really want to hear what you have to say and your words are ignored.

Remember:

There is no greater setback than being drained by an unsupportive and difficult person. They don't complete what they start.

Their manipulative and judgmental nature makes them very dangerous.

Watch out for their distractions—they're a major setback.

Identify the kinds of people you associate with and rid yourself of them, as they may influence your actions, and let them throw the stones, the stones will make you stronger.

In order to achieve successful results in your life, surround yourself with positive people.

When you deal with toxic people, set limits for them and only help them when and if possible. Don't allow them to steal your time. Sometimes we tell people too much, and they may be jealous, they can plot and put stumbling blocks in your way.

Distance yourself from their behavior by recognizing them from the start.

Another Key Factor—Burning Bridges

Be very careful with the relationships you have with others and never make promises you can't do or keep.

Always keep a positive attitude towards everyone.

Sometimes, people who were rude towards people turn out to be the very person they needed for a crucial situation.

No matter who it is in your life, whether a close friend, a family member, your business partner or someone new, always establish a good relationship and maintain it.

It will take you a long way, who knows they may have information that could be beneficial to you as well.

Additionally, it's the best way to conduct our lives since we reap what we sow, good or bad.

Plant the seeds of good every day of your life. You'll reap a harvest of good coming back!

Unexpected Setbacks

My heart really goes out to people that may be in this situation that had an unexpected setback.

Things like sickness, death, losing a job, or losing a business fall into this category.

Now losing a job or losing a business can be resolved overtime.

But losing a family friend or loved one due to death can be very painful and traumatic.

I recently lost two of my sisters, one year apart, my pastor, and another minister, and friends that I love.

So, I understand that kind of grief and pain, I'm still getting over it. And I send my condolences for anyone in that situation.

Sickness is usually treatable with the right doctors, medications, or surgeries, but most of the time, I would say it's because of our poor eating habits, what we're consuming.

A lot of sickness can be prevented, so we should really study our bodies and find out more about the vitamins and nutrients we need, and why.

We need to make sure that we're eating the correct foods, the right oils, and staying away from sugar and high carbohydrates. There's tons of information on the web that teaches us about eating properly.

I personally listen to Bobby Approved on YouTube, referred by a good friend. He has a lot of information on eating the right foods, and he gives you a good education on why these foods are so important and what to eat. He takes you on a virtual shopping spree with him, pointing out what you should avoid. Maybe check him out.

In terms of our health and eating habits, we should really pay attention to this part since a lot of our illnesses can be prevented if we pay attention to what we eat.

This also could be a major setback.

Remember you're on a mission.

Quiz

- What is a setback?
- How can we prevent setbacks from happening?
- Give two main points on how to identify toxic people in your life.
- Why should we never burn Bridges?
- What are some setback key points to remember?

Fear Is Another Form of Setback

Our greatest enemy is fear. It's something we must conquer because it grips our minds and cripples us. And we must master it in order to overcome that power.

What are your fears when it comes to your plans or your destiny?

Fear for some may be getting started, the fear of failure, or not knowing enough to succeed. In order to achieve your goals, you must educate yourself on the topic matter, because there are answers all around you.

Additionally, there's a fear of rejection. We all have fears, but if you can overcome that fear, your gift and passion will prevail.

For example, if you are deciding how to market a product or service, then find out who needs it and provide it for them.

Find the Need and Fill It

In other words, find your target market, their interests, the age group of who you'll be marketing to. Taking action and learning how to deal with fear will diminish the fear, no matter what it is.

You can learn more about these topics on our upcoming business talk show *Irayah*, coming to IBCN on Roku, TCL, Local Now, Herugotv, and other major networks.

It will also be listed on our site, www.ibcntv.com.

My First Experience of Fear in Business

When I first got started in business, I remember opening a business to deliver disposal diapers in our local neighborhoods. It was after a major earthquake, when this service was really needed.

After asking myself the best way to accomplish this, I got a team. We knocked on doors, but no one wanted them. I begin to get fearful that it wasn't going to work. So we put the boxes on the street corner that day, and people started coming from everywhere. Even the bus driver stopped to pick up cases.

I'll never know what the difference was between knocking on the door versus putting them out on the street, unless God intervened.

This is a great example of not missing your moment and finding the need and filling it.

There are a lot of things we have to try until it works. Thankfully, it only took us two tries, but the point was, we didn't give up; we tried something else, and it worked.

It would have been really easy to give up. In fact, it was so successful we couldn't keep up with the demand. They were asking what else we had to offer.

I was encouraged to keep going by results like these, and you'll be encouraged when you see your results as well.

Remember all of your success and failures, because it will help you.

What Is Fear?

It's an unpleasant feeling triggered by the perception of danger real or imagination.

Be careful of your fear triggers and identify what is causing that fear.

Realizing it's our greatest enemy.

It is best not to discard or abandon something out of fear that you may be close to achieving it.

Don't allow it to depress you and never allow yourself to get in situations to trigger that fear.

In my research I found that fear is one of the seven universal emotions experienced by everyone.

Example: I recommend taking a swimming lesson if you're afraid of drowning so that you can face your fear head-on.

When I first performed before a crowd, it was scary. However, I overcame my fear by looking above the crowd's heads and focusing on the back wall until the crowd began to accept me.

Think positive thoughts and visualize yourself doing it. Just be yourself. We get fearful when we try to be or do something like someone else. As long as you're being yourself, this should calm you down.

And find other ways of doing something that's comfortable for you.

Don't allow your disappointments or minor setbacks to cause you to fear something. It may look like a setback when it may actually be a blessing in disguise.

Be aware of your setbacks, but don't live in denial of them. Having faith in the future and having a positive attitude should drive away your fears because, if you think about it, it's really not as bad as you think.

Never allow fear to grip your mind.

There have seen times when I thought I was in a fearful situation, and it turned out that it wasn't bad at all, and it wasn't like I thought it would be—it was so easy.

So, if we can move the obstacle of fear, we will be surprised how much we can thrive.

Fear is a true enemy!

> Fear thou not; for I am with thee: be not dismayed; for I am thy God: I will strengthen thee; yea, I will help thee; yea, I will uphold thee with the right hand of my righteousness. (Isaiah 41:10)

Quiz

- What is fear?
- What is our greatest enemy?
- What do you do if you have the fear of failure to succeed?
- What would happen to your fear once you know what to do?

Chapter 8

UTILIZE YOUR
SUPPORT SYSTEM

𝒴OU'RE ON A PATH TO your destiny, so don't forget the help around you. It might be a friend, a workshop, a seminar, a business networking group, a book, or television. The process of seeking help or feeling overwhelmed can be challenging, but it will be manageable if you seek the right guidance and pray for it.

> Where no counsel is the people fall; but in the multitude of counsellors there is safety. (Proverbs 11:14)

So, be attentive to the signs around you. Sometimes we miss the answers that are right in front of us if we don't pay attention to them.

When you're in conversation with someone, you never know when you'll hear the answer. Someone might have information you need or a missing piece that you need to get to the next level.

Even a child may have the answer. Just one word or praise or sentence could be the very answer you're looking for, and that's a wonderful thing to find.

You see, those signals are helpful to you as well as you just need to pay attention until it become natural to you.

If you seek advice from someone about your plans, it's important to be open to their suggestions; sometimes their advice will be useful or maybe it won't work for your circumstance, so pay attention to what they are saying.

The alternative is to take what you need from the conversation and spit out the rest, using what you need now or at a later time or advising someone else.

In listening to that person, you never know which advice they may have in the future, what connections they may have, or what you may be able to offer them.

Iron Sharpens Iron

> Iron sharpeneth iron; so a man sharpeneth the countenance of his friend. (Proverbs 27:17 KJV)

I believe we are here on this planet to accomplish our mission and impart knowledge to others, while achieving our own goals.

What Does It Mean to Utilize Your Support System?

To utilize means to make practical and effective use of.

And support means to bear all or part of the weight of; to hold up.

(Definitions from Oxford Languages)

What does this mean?

As a result of having a supportive network, you'll be able to improve your goals and reduce stress and anxiety since you won't have to bear the burden alone.

What A Support System Does

You can ask them for feedback on your ideas and your goals your next move. They can share with you some of their experiences, mistakes, and successes regarding certain issues that may help you avoid many pitfalls. They can become great mentors for you.

They can inspire you when you're feeling down and not feeling motivated, and they can help you spiritually physically and sometimes financially. We all need a mentor and a support system, whether in business or personal.

In my life, I've been blessed with many mentors, many ministers who spoke in my life, many businesspeople who gave me great advice, many elderly people who helped me mature, and the greatest one has been my mom, who helped me be the best woman I could be.

And my dad who nourished and inspired me, my children who motivate me and remind me of how grateful they are to have me as their mom.

All of these are examples of support systems because they kept you motivated, they keep you focused, and when they speak to you, you feel as though you have to live up to what they said because it has been spoken into the atmosphere.

Maintaining a positive environment is awesome!

So we must utilize our support system because they want to be there and help you, they want to pour into your life; it's part of their assignment as well.

The person you are fortunate to have in your life is there to bear part or all of the weight and to uphold you; be thankful for this if you have one of them, because there are many people who don't.

If you don't have it, surround yourself with positive people from organizations, churches, or groups meetings who share your goals. This is also part of a support system.

Embrace this it will take you a long way!

- Always show your appreciation and make sure those who are in your support system know how much you care, honor them, and appreciate them.
- Always be available for them as well. Stay connected to them.
- Communication should always be open, and assistance should always be accepted.

This wouldn't be complete without mentioning the most important element of your support system, which is self-awareness, the ability to understand how your actions, thoughts, and emotions align with your internal values.

More Key Points to Remember

Do what you have to do now, because time is passing every day.

Don't worry if you don't have the experience or knowledge in your field. Educate yourself to sharpen your skills.

Try not to wear too many hats, and don't stress yourself out. You can always outsource your services, find experts in those areas of your project to help you bring it to fruition, and you'll discover you're also learning while you're doing it.

The point is don't give up and don't quit, because time waits for no one, and before you know it, so much time has passed by and you haven't done a thing while living in regrets.

So no matter how old you are now, don't think that it's too late because it's never too late to get started and win. Get started as soon as possible.

Remember: Things are changing every day. Trends are changing. People are changing. So make sure you are keeping up with the change.

You got this. Your gift will make room for you, and it's just waiting for you to use it.

> A man's gift maketh room for him, and bringeth him before great men. (Proverbs 18:16 KJV)

Consider everything around you as a lesson or an idea or an instruction; glean from the positive people in your circle.

Everything has a voice if you just pay attention you'll find answers in the most common and simple places that you would never imagine.

An old saying is that a child would lead them. You would be surprised how a child can say one little small thing that sparks an idea in you. Or provides a missing piece to the puzzle you were struggling with.

Life is so amazing!

It's my belief that God does not leave us without answers.

He said in Matthew 7:7,"Ask and it shall be given, seek and you shall find, knock and the door shall be open unto you."

We wouldn't have to worry about anything if we followed these principles, which seem so simple.

The answers are within you, the answers are around you, and the answers are waiting to be discovered for you.

In my opinion, it's quite troubling that people can be so jealous of other people, because if they really got to know them and found out how they think and approach life, they would learn how to glean from them and be able to help each other succeed.

You never know what they had to endure to get where they are until they share their stories with you. You'll be able to appreciate them more. And you'll discover many great things for yourself just by rubbing shoulders with them and being in their presence.

You would be doing yourself a disservice if you didn't at least get to know the person and dig deep within yourself to find the hidden jewel within it. It may shock you!

Sometime we can cut off our blessings by doing such things. If you see someone that you admire, get to know them, find out their struggles, and they may even give you some insights on what you can do with yours.

Don't block or hinder your blessings by being envious or jealous. There's no need because you have something great in you as well that's yet to be seen and discovered.

Never stop learning. Always be teachable and coachable.

Your destiny is waiting for you!

You got this. Your gift is making room for you, and it's just waiting for you to use it.

Quiz

- Why is it good to pay attention to your surroundings?
- What does it mean to utilize your support system?
- What does it mean to never give up?
- Why is it important to show your appreciation?
- Why should we utilize our support system?

Chapter 9

A PURPOSE WAITING
FOR DESTINY

*D*ON'T LET YOUR HEAD DREAM take over your life. The longer you sit on it and think about it, the longer it will take to manifest. Just do it. You'll learn as you go.

In some cases, if you aren't careful, you can have a dream for so long that it appears in your mind that it's already happening, because you're still nursing it when in fact it has not yet begun to manifest.

Family and friends will hear you talk about it constantly, but when they look at you, they see someone totally different.

Their eyes are not open to what you see, nor can they understand what you're saying; so it seems as if it doesn't fit you.

It's like a joke to them, because you're always talking about things you've never done or will ever do, and many times it's so big they can't visualize you achieving them.

You have to make it happen.

Whenever you're stuck, don't be afraid to ask for help.

Find a mentor, learn your craft, and know it inside and out.

There are times when things you think you want are just the opposite of what they should be, so you need to be crystal clear about your vision.

Identify your vision and ask yourself why you want to do this and what purpose it will serve.

This is how to you reach your destiny to understanding your purpose.

Is this a genuine desire on your part, or did you get the idea from someone else?

There is a lot to learn about you by asking yourself these questions. You don't want to be walking in someone else's shoes. Stay in your lane and on your own path,

Since you have experienced what others haven't, your paths will be different from others because they haven't gone through what you have, so they won't see things the way you do—your strategies will be different.

Embrace your passion and drive the road to your success, because your experiences have trained and equipped for this. You're now ready to go above and beyond your expectations. You have to own it!

It's Never Okay to Take a Day Off

When I say it's never okay to take a day off, that doesn't mean you need to work all the time. I just mean that you should not get too relaxed doing the ordinary things to the point where you stop focusing on your purpose. Thus, when I say, don't take a day off, I mean that you should put something into practice that will assist you in achieving your goal.

You should always aim to stay on track, and the best way to do that is to put that goal into action every single day.

Remember: your destiny is waiting for you.

One of the great fun ways could be just staying fit, because when we're in good health, it keeps us on our toes and keeps us alert to think properly.

If we feel worn out and tired and don't get enough nutrients in our body, we might feel overwhelmed, and we'll have no desire to accomplish anything that day.

While taking a day off, keep your mind on positive thoughts and the right people in your circle, reflect on your goals, and work on your plans so that you stay on track. You may want to take a walk, watch what you eat, or just browse your notes, because your goal is to stay focused.

These are things that you do can do in the pursuit of your purpose. Everything counts. I always love to say God doesn't waste anything—he can use it. Your success could be long term but be willing to work on it step by step and wait because you'll get there.

Aspirations versus Affirmation

What is the difference between aspirations and affirmation?

At first glance, the words "aspiration" and "affirmation" may appear similar. However, aspiration refers to a desire or ambition to achieve something. According to research by The National Institute of Health, there are two main types of aspirations:

1. Intrinsic aspirations are those that fulfill physiological needs and contribute to an individual's well-being.

2. Extrinsic aspirations are those that focus on achieving external goals, such as wealth or fame. These goals can sometimes negatively impact well-being and divert resources away from intrinsic aspirations.

Aim high to achieve your goals and always consider what will be the next step. Overachieving and ambition is described as striving to be the best you can be. Don't overdo it.

However, affirmation is the action or process of affirming something or being affirmed to offer someone emotional support or encouragement, and these are ways that you can affirm yourself with aspiration and affirmation.

You know the old saying is sometimes we have to encourage ourselves because we may not have someone around us that would encourage us.

Each morning, you should tell yourself these affirmations, which could give you the aspiration to become the best you've ever been to achieve your greatest potential.

Keep saying these words in your everyday life affirmations until you have said them so often you start believing them. The environment around you will become more positive, and your goals will be attainable.

Daily Affirmations

- I am successful, confident, and powerful.
- I am stronger and getting better and better every day.
- All that I need God has placed inside of me.
- I am highly favored, and I am an unstoppable force of nature.
- I am a breathing example of motivation and inspiration to help others.
- I live in abundance and focused on my plans and abilities.
- I won't let my past rob me of my future.
- I am having a positive and inspiring impact on the people I come into contact today.
- I'm rising above the thoughts that would try to make me angry or afraid.
- Today is a phenomenal day because ...
- I have a second chance to make a first impression.

Please note: I would also suggest looking in your KJV Bible to get more affirmations; and I recommend Dr. Cindy Trimms's book *Commanding Your Morning*.

Quiz

- What is your destiny and purpose?
- Have you identified your vision?
- What steps have you taken towards your vision?
- Are you ready to walk in your purpose and destiny?
- What is your next step?

You will be more ready to answer these questions in the next chapter of your success.

Chapter 10

PERFECTION

$\mathcal{P}$ERFECTION: THE STATE OR QUALITY of being free or as free as possible from flaws or defects.

(Definition from Oxford Languages)

A lack of perfection is said to steal people's confidence. Some of the most successful people in the world didn't make it there by being perfect but by being themselves and embracing their gifts. They have something that someone needed that would add value to their lives.

Don't worry about being perfect, but you should always perfect your worth by doing everything in the spirit of excellence.

You are more appreciated when people see that you love what you do and that you are not money driven.

This is how they know you care about their needs. I would rather spend more money on a product or service if I see the owner understands good customer service and care for their clients. Having these qualities and characteristics should be your company and personal standards.

There's no way to hide it because even your body language and tone of voice will reveal a lot about you; wherever you go, you'll take yourself with you, so always be careful what you do.

Dress appropriately for the occasion. People notice everything, from your hair to your shoes. If just one thing is off, it could ruin a deal or contract. You shouldn't overdress or underdress. And always be on time.

This shouldn't be necessary to mention, but please pay attention to your personal hygiene.

If you're having a bad day, it's better to cancel your meeting than to just show up with a bad attitude, or if you've resolved that issue beforehand and have a positive attitude now, you can go in with a good attitude, because people can sense these things.

Getting the Approval of Others

We spent a lot of time trying to impress others to be validated by them when the fact of the matter could be that they're trying to impress you as well, to get you to look up to them.

So despite the phony world we live in, sometimes we all need to just be ourselves instead of concealing what makes us unique, and stop walking in the shadow of others.

If we could just be who we really are, we'll discover a person the world has never seen, one whom God has made unique. He told Jeremiah,

> Before I formed you in the belly I knew thee; and before thou comest forth out of the womb I sanctified thee, and I ordained thee a prophet to the nations. (Jeremiah 1:5 KJV)

And until this day, even though Jeremiah is no longer on the earth with us, he is still a prophet to the nations.

Now what has God ordained you to do, because it's generational, and it's too big. You won't live long enough to carry it out.

The mantle would be passed to the next generation, but you have to start and bring it forth. Remember your destiny is waiting for you and God is depending on you to birth it, for a second chance to make a first impression is something only God can do for you.

My Belief System

Everyone should have a belief system; this is where your faith comes from to keep you pressing on. As a result of all the wonderful experiences I've had in my life, I've witnessed so many great things.

When you get to the point where you believe in yourself and the abilities that God has placed inside of you, nothing will be hard for you to do believe or accomplish.

Here is a scripture that I live by, and I stand on it with all my might, because I believe it to be so, and it has proven to be real in my life:

> For verily I say unto you, That whosoever shall say unto this mountain, Be thou removed, and be thou cast into the sea; and shall not doubt in his heart, but shall believe that those things which he saith shall come to pass; he shall have whatsoever he saith.
>
> Therefore I say unto you, What things soever ye desire, when ye pray, believe

that ye receive them, and ye shall have them. (Mark 11:23–24)

Some of you who are reading this book may or may not believe there's a God, but for me to tell you anything different in my walk and my purpose to destiny would be a lie.

I have to give credit where credit is due, and it's to my Lord and Savior Jesus Christ. Yes, this is my belief system.

There are many of us who may have things in our lives that can make us not feel worthy of walking in our destiny and purpose.

It can be the lack of education, or appearance, or income, or age, but let me be the first to tell you, if someone have never said this to you before:

You are worthy, and you are more than enough.

Why? It's because of your uniqueness that you're the only one like you in this world.

What will we do without you?

We just haven't met you yet.

We are yearning for you, but we don't know who you are.

We need you—we're missing you.

We are disappointed because we can't find you.

Why are we feeling this way?

We didn't understand until you showed up, but now

we understand that it was you who brought us the peace we were missing. So you see you're worthy, and you're good enough for a whole world that's waiting for you, somewhere to connect with your destiny. Remember: your destiny is still looking for you.

There may be other reasons why a person may feel he or she needs to be perfect to get that second chance to make a first impression,

Maybe something happened in your life where you feel that life dealt you the wrong deck of cards. Maybe you were abandoned or abused, or maybe in prison wrongfully accused, but whatever it is, there's still hope if you can believe.

Someone very close to me served many years in prison, but while he was there, he took upholstery training, and later, he got a job there where he was monitored to work in that field.

In fact, he became so good at it that he opened his own business when he returned home, and soon secured contracts with restaurants, other businesses, and individuals who needed his services. And he bought his own home while running his business.

That was his second chance to make a good first impression, and he succeeded.

The guidelines in this book will help some of you to avoid making bad decisions that can derail your destinies and progress, as I did.

I may not be able to show you how to handle some things, but God does. Despite feeling like you might have missed out, you'll see that there's still hope, like it was for me, that your ship has just arrived because now you realize you still have a chance to overcome and fulfill the purpose that God has for you.

And I'll ask you again: What is that burning desire inside of you that won't leave you alone? Well just reach for it, because it's closer than you think. You've been prepared for this, it's inside of you, your second chance to make a first impression.

Walking In My Destiny

Little did I know that during the struggles with the ups and downs in my life that God was shaping and molding me. I didn't understand that this was what it would take to pull greatness out of me. I didn't understand how he was using my enemies to push me into my destiny.

I didn't understand that when I became homeless, there was something in it God could use in my life. I didn't understand that the things that I have gone through was for my good. Yes, I was one of those people who had toxic people in my life. I was one of those people who had a lot of great opportunities to past me by.

I was one of those people who was concerned about being rejected. I was one of those people who had big dreams that I thought I couldn't achieve. Yes, I was one of those people, but I'm not anymore since I found my strength, and my greatest strength came from the Lord.

Many prophesies was spoken over my life that had taken so long to manifest, but I believe it took that long because I wasn't ready, and when I became ready, it was waiting for me.

My hope is that this book helps you to find what is waiting for you. I'm not quite where I need to be, but I'm not in the place I was.

Today I can say that part of my dreams have come true. One was to finish this book, and the other is that I have my own broadcast network, IBCN—a free family network broadcast that's now on Roku, Local Now, TCL, Herogotv, and counting.

I'm also working on another talk show, a business talk show, *Irayah,* and maybe by the time you get this book, it will be airing. This journey has not been easy, but it has been rewarding. The greatest thing for me now is to look back at the things that I believed God for, and that was spoken over my life.

And now I can look back and see it in manifestation, such as turning on my TV and watching my channel. I can go to the bookstore and see this book on shelves and on Amazon.

And you can do it too. Whatever your dreams or goals are, whether you think it's small or big, it can and it will happen if you follow at least some of the guidelines in this book.

You would get there. Just believe in yourself and have faith. Love yourself enough and give yourself the opportunity to prove to your doubters wrong. You can do this, and I'm here for you if you have any questions you can always reach me through my website, www.ibcntv.com.

I also invite you to watch my upcoming talk show, *Irayah*, that will soon be seen on IBCN and the other networks I mentioned above, also on YouTube.

See you at the top. Do something that no one has ever done. You got this!

Quiz

- What is perfection?
- Why should we have a good character?
- Do you think you seek approval from others?
- Do you have a belief system?
- Do you think you have something great that will add value to someone's life?

90

Printed in the United States
by Baker & Taylor Publisher Services